Super Fun Facts For Curious Kids

You Gotta Be Kidding!!

Fascinating Facts About History, Holidays, Science, Traveling, And More

By David W. Leon

Written by David W. Leon
Illustrated by Rhiannon Perrin

Table of Contents

Introduction

I grew up absorbed in trivia books, I loved watching Jeopardy in the afternoons, and I signed up for way too many email subscriptions just to get their daily trivia email blasts. One thing I noticed with trivia books lately is that the newer books seem to be falling flat, and upon further research, it seems I'm not the only person who has seen this unfortunate shift.

- Instead of being easy to read, now most trivia books are overwhelmingly text intensive with minimal or no visuals.
- Instead of providing unique or obscure facts, now most trivia books regurgitate the same information.
- Instead of being age appropriate, now some trivia books swing widely from appropriate facts to unexpectedly dark facts.

I've decided to try my hand at solving the above issues and created a new way to engage with the trivia!

If you're like me and love to have fun while learning about crazy and quirky facts, then I might just have the solution for you.

I hope you enjoy!

Level 1
Bet I Can Stump You

Questions 1-20

Discover Something New About This Whacky World We Live In!

Be Sure To Share What You've Learned With Others!

Super Fun Facts
For Curious Kids

Question 1

What is the name of the festival of lights celebrated by the Hindu, Sikh, and Jain faiths?

a) Mawlid

b) Diwali

c) Lohri

d) Ram Navami

David W. Leon
Fun Facts Books

Answer 1

Because it is celebrated all over the world by different faiths, Diwali is also known as Diwali or Deepavali. Although each celebration is slightly different, the holiday celebrates the triumph of good over evil. Candles and diyas, clay lamps, are lit to light up the darkness. In India, Diwali is usually a five-day celebration whereas other places dedicate one day to this festival of lights.

Super Fun Facts
For Curious Kids

Question 2

What Seattle landmark was built for the 1962 Century 21 Exposition?

a) Sky Views Observatory

b) The Space Needle

c) Chief Seattle Sculpture

d) Pioneer Park

David W. Leon
Fun Facts Books

Answer 2

Edward E. Nelson designed the UFO-shaped Space Needle for the space-themed Century 21 Exposition. The Space Needle is 605 feet tall and offers a 360-view of Seattle from its three main viewing rooms.

Super Fun Facts
For Curious Kids

Question 3

What animal is immune to snake venom?

a) Mongoose

b) Beaver

c) Duck

d) Rat

Answer 3

Mongooses, particularly the Indian gray mongoose, are well-known for their ability to fend off and kill venomous snakes, including cobras. They exhibit quick reflexes, agility, and a thick coat of fur that provides some protection against snake bites.

Super Fun Facts
For Curious Kids

Question 4

What was the official language of the Roman Empire?

a) Arabic

b) Italian

c) Latin

d) Romance language

David W. Leon
Fun Facts Books

Answer 4

The official language of the Roman Empire was Latin. The territory of the Empire was extensive and ruled over hundreds of different peoples. Although they obeyed the Roman government, they had their own languages and cultures. However, the laws and taxes were conveyed in Latin.

Super Fun Facts
For Curious Kids

Question 5

What is the name of Peru's annual Festival of the Sun?

a) Fiesta de la Candelaria

b) Fiesta de las Cruces

c) Fiesta de la Virgen del Carmen

d) Inti Raymi

David W. Leon
Fun Facts Books

Answer 5

Originally an ancient Incan festival, today's Inti Raymi features actors reenacting the Incan religious ceremony in front of the Coricancha, a sun temple. The ceremony takes place on June 24th each year, during the Winter Solstice in the southern hemisphere.

Super Fun Facts
For Curious Kids

Question 6

Which London landmark is inscribed with the Latin phrase Domine Salvam Fasc Reginam Nostram Victoriam Primam ("O Lord, keep safe our Queen Victoria the First")?

a) Big Ben

b) The Shard

c) St. Paul's Cathedral

d) Royal Albert Hall

David W. Leon
Fun Facts Books

Answer 6

England's House of Parliament and Elizabeth Tower are more commonly known as Big Ben. This inscription can be found on the face of the clock. Although the name Big Ben has come to refer to both the Parliament Building and Elizabeth Tower, it was originally the nickname of the clock's massive bell.

Super Fun Facts
For Curious Kids

Question 7

Which animal kills the most humans every year?

a) Sharks

b) Bears

c) Coyotes

d) Mosquitoes

Answer 7

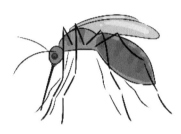

Mosquitoes cause an estimated 725,000 human deaths a year - vastly more than any other animal. While they may seem small and harmless individually, mosquitoes are responsible for transmitting several deadly diseases, including malaria, dengue fever, Zika virus, and yellow fever. These diseases collectively cause millions of deaths each year, predominantly in tropical and subtropical regions where mosquito-borne illnesses are prevalent.

Super Fun Facts
For Curious Kids

Question 8

Athens and Sparta were the two main polis in ancient Greece, but they were enemies. There was a great war between them. What was it called?

a) Napoleonic Wars

b) The Crusades

c) The Peloponnesian War

d) Wars of the Roses

David W. Leon
Fun Facts Books

Answer 8

Athens was one of the most powerful polis, the independent cities of ancient Greece. The Peloponesse was the southern region in Greece that included Sparta, a militarily organized city-state. Athenians recognized the threat and initiated the so-called Peloponnesian War against the Spartans to win supremacy.

Super Fun Facts
For Curious Kids

Question 9

What is the name of the largest and most famous Peruvian festival?

a) Fiesta de la Candelaria

b) Festival Internacional de la Vendimia

c) Fiesta de las Cruces

d) Mistura Culinary Festival

David W. Leon
Fun Facts Books

Answer 9

Not only is it the largest festival in Peru, but the Fiesta de la Candelaria is one of the largest in South America. Celebrating the Virgin of Candelaria, the festival is held in Puno, her birthplace.

Super Fun Facts
For Curious Kids

Question 10

What dome has been preserved as a ruin in the Japanese city of Hiroshima?

a) Genbaku Dome

b) Dome of the Rock

c) Hagia Sophia

d) St. Basil's Cathedral

Answer 10

Found in the Hiroshima Peace Memorial, the Genbaku Dome was the only structure left standing after the atomic bomb was dropped on August 6, 1945. Japan decided not to rebuild the area around the dome and converted it into a memorial park in honor of the victims and as an eternal reminder of the need for world peace.

Super Fun Facts
For Curious Kids

Question 11

In 1968, geomorphologist Jim Bowlern discovered what 40,000-year-old remains in Australia?

a) Mungo Lady

b) Lucy

c) Richard III

d) Cleopatra

Answer 11

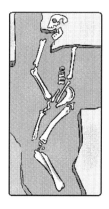

Mungo Lady was discovered in a shallow grave in the Willandra Lakes region of New South Wales, Australia. Mungo Lady is estimated to be approximately 42,000 years old, making it one of the oldest anatomically modern human remains in Australia.

Super Fun Facts
For Curious Kids

Question 12

Where did the Pilgrims come from?

a) England

b) Iceland

c) America

d) Canada

Answer 12

The Pilgrims were English immigrants compelled to flee due to religious motives. In the 17th century, after spending time in the Netherlands, they arrived in Plymouth Harbor and settled as a colony. A pilgrim is a person who has to migrate for a religious or moral purpose.

Super Fun Facts
For Curious Kids

Question 13

What is the name of the Finnish holiday where the last person to wake up has water thrown over their head?

a) Laskiainen

b) Pääsiäinen

c) Juhannus

d) Unikeonpäivä

David W. Leon
Fun Facts Books

Answer 13

On July 27th, which in Finland is called Unikeonpäivä or "National Sleepyhead Day," the last person asleep is dubbed the "laziest" in the house and awakened by having water thrown over their head. Naantali, a city of southwest Finland, celebrates this holiday by throwing a celebrity into the sea at 7 a.m. each year.

Super Fun Facts
For Curious Kids

Question 14

What artist created the marble and bronze statue known as "The Thinker?"

a) Pablo Picasso

b) Donatello

c) Auguste Rodin

d) Camille Claudel

David W. Leon
Fun Facts Books

Answer 14

Originally called "The Poet," Auguste Rodin's "The Thinker" is in the gardens of the Rodin Museum, Paris. Rodin made several versions of this sculpture, but the most famous version is a six-foot statue of a male nude thinking pensively.

Super Fun Facts
For Curious Kids

Question 15

What is the scientific word for nearsightedness, meaning you can't see far away?

a) Blindness

b) Hyperopia

c) Myopia

d) Cataracts

David W. Leon
Fun Facts Books

Answer 15

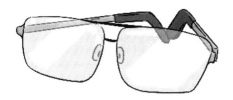

Myopia, commonly known as nearsightedness, is a problem where distant objects appear blurry, but close-up objects can be seen clearly. It occurs when the eyeball is slightly longer than normal or when the cornea (the clear front part of the eye) is too curved, causing the incoming light to focus in front of the retina instead of directly on it.

Super Fun Facts
For Curious Kids

Question 16

The Pilgrims made a long journey across the Atlantic Ocean in 1660. What was the name of the ship that took them to America?

a) The Speedwell

b) The Mayflower

c) The Santa Maria

d) The Royal Catherine

Answer 16

The Pilgrims crossed the Atlantic Ocean from England to Virginia in a ship called the Mayflower. Originally, they had rented two ships, but the second leaked. The Mayflower departed on September 6, 1620, with 120 passengers. Some of them couldn't board.

Super Fun Facts
For Curious Kids

Question 17

What item do Dutch children leave out for Sinterklaas to fill with presents or candy?

a) Stockings

b) Shoes

c) Hats

d) Purses

Answer 17

Children leave their shoes out for Sinterklaas, a Dutch version of Saint Nicholas, to be filled on December 5th. On December 5th, children and adults sing popular songs about Sinterklaas, some of them dating back to the 19th-century.

Super Fun Facts
For Curious Kids

Question 18

In what museum would you see a replica of Pink Floyd's "The Wall?"

a) EMP Museum

b) The Rock & Roll Hall of Fame

c) Grammy Museum

d) National Music Museum

David W. Leon
Fun Facts Books

Answer 18

On the fourth floor of the Rock & Roll Hall of Fame Museum in Cleveland, Ohio, visitors can see a complete replica of Pink Floyd's stage from their 1990 performance of their album "The Wall" in Germany. Honoring Cleveland for the city's profound influence on the popularity of rock & roll music, the museum houses many rock & roll artifacts. Each year the Rock & Roll Hall of Fame inducts musicians and bands for their contributions to the music world.

Super Fun Facts
For Curious Kids

Question 19

What is the name of the units used to measure electrical power?

a) Watts

b) Quasar

c) Doppler

d) Escape Velocity

Answer 19

Named after James Watts, the inventor of the steam engine, electricity is measured in watts. The watt is a very small measurement of power, while the power consumption of large devices is measured in terms of kilowatts, megawatts, or gigawatts.

Super Fun Facts
For Curious Kids

Question 20

Which of these European nations helped the United States in the Revolutionary War?

a) Spain

b) England

c) France

d) Italy

Answer 20

Originally, the 13 colonies belonged to the English empire. France, England's historical enemy, took advantage of the war to help the colonialist and, in the process, weaken the English nation. Therefore, the French king provided the revolutionaries with weapons, ammunition, troops, and naval support.

Level 2
Wow The Crowd With Your Intellect

Questions 21-40

Stay Curious!

To Quote Frank Zappa:

"A Mind Is Like A Parachute. It Doesn't Work If It Is Not Open."

Super Fun Facts
For Curious Kids

Question 21

What holiday originated in Mexico but is now more popular in the United States?

a) Día de la Bandera (Flag Day)

b) Día de Reyes (Epiphany/Three Kings Day)

c) Cinco de Mayo (Fifth of May)

d) Día del Trabajo (Labor Day)

David W. Leon
Fun Facts Books

Answer 21

On May 5, 1862, Mexican troops defeated French invaders in Puebla, Mexico. Now recognized as Cinco de Mayo, there are regional celebrations, but it is widely celebrated throughout the United States to recognize the contributions of Mexican culture to America.

Super Fun Facts
For Curious Kids

Question 22

While many American cities celebrate "Oktoberfest," in what German city is the original annual festival?

a) Berlin

b) Hamburg

c) Meine

d) Munich

David W. Leon
Fun Facts Books

Answer 22

This famous beer festival originated in the city of Munich on October 12, 1810, to celebrate the marriage of the crown prince of Bavaria. Today, the mayor of Munich always opens the first keg, which kicks off the annual beer festival, where roughly two million gallons of beer are drunk every year.

Super Fun Facts
For Curious Kids

Question 23

Where on Earth did Nasa test the Mars rover before sending it into space?

a) Atacama Desert

b) White Sands, New Mexico

c) The Grand Canyon

d) The Sahara Desert

Answer 23

NASA used the Atacama Desert in Chile as a testing ground due to its resemblance to the harsh and arid conditions of Mars. The desert's extreme dryness, high altitude, and lack of vegetation makes it a suitable location for testing rover prototypes.

Super Fun Facts
For Curious Kids

Question 24

According to the most accepted theories, how did human beings arrive in North America in prehistoric times?

a) Crossed an ice bridge from Russia to Alaska

b) Sailed the Pacific Ocean from Polynesia

c) Sailed from Iceland to Greenland

d) They came from South America

David W. Leon
Fun Facts Books

Answer 24

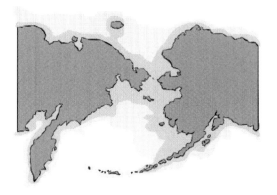

The most accepted theory is that the first humans arrived in America by crossing from Siberia in eastern Russia to Alaska. They didn't sail across the ocean, but walked across an icy bridge in the Bering Strait. About 10,000 years ago, there was an Ice Age and the extremely low temperatures froze the ocean.

Super Fun Facts
For Curious Kids

Question 25

What holiday is now considered America's second Independence Day?

a) Juneteenth

b) Veteran's Day

c) Labor Day

d) Lincoln's Birthday

Answer 25

While the Emancipation Proclamation was issued on January 1, 1863, not all slaves were immediately freed in the United States. It would take two and a half years for the slaves in Texas to receive news that they were free. In 1866, a year after slavery ended in Texas, the newly free people celebrated with a "Jubilee Day" on June 19th, which became known as "Juneteenth." President Biden made it a national holiday on June 17, 2021.

Super Fun Facts
For Curious Kids

Question 26

Which British author lived in a now famous home in Lodsworth, West Sussex, England?

a) E.H. Shepard

b) Virginia Woolf

c) Charles Dickens

d) Bram Stoker

David W. Leon
Fun Facts Books

Answer 26

E.H. Shepard, children's book author and illustrator who wrote The Wind in the Willows and Winnie-the-Pooh, lived in Lodsworth, England. The brick house which sits at the end of the street was named in his honor, and draws many literary lovers each year.

Super Fun Facts
For Curious Kids

Question 27

How many miles per hour can neurons in the human brain travel throughout the body?

a) 75 mph

b) 10 mph

c) 25 mph

d) 200 mph

David W. Leon
Fun Facts Books

Answer 27

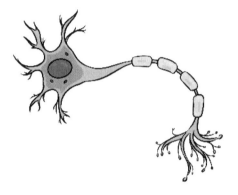

Neurons transmit information to your brain at speeds exceeding 150 miles (241 kilometers) per hour, and your brain employs motor neurons to quickly send a response back. Motor neurons are capable of relaying messages at speeds surpassing 200 miles (322 kilometers) per hour.

Super Fun Facts
For Curious Kids

Question 28

The Portuguese were the first after the Spanish to cross the Atlantic Ocean and search for colonies in South America. Which current country belonged to the Portuguese empire in the 16th century?

a) Mexico

b) Jamaica

c) Brazil

d) Uruguay

David W. Leon
Fun Facts Books

Answer 28

The Portuguese were the first to venture across the ocean and, in the 16th century, also took possession of colonies in the recently discovered continent. They searched for new navigational routes to avoid the Ottomans in the Mediterranean Sea. First, they traveled along the African shores and later crossed the Atlantic to establish a colony in current Brazil.

Super Fun Facts
For Curious Kids

Question 29

What United States holiday celebrates the planting and preservation of trees?

a) Earth Day

b) Arbor Day

c) Houseplant Appreciation Day

d) National Gardening Day

David W. Leon
Fun Facts Books

Answer 29

Made a national holiday by President Nixon, Arbor Day falls on the last Friday of April. The Latin word for tree is "arbor," so the day literally translates to "Tree Day."

Super Fun Facts
For Curious Kids

Question 30

After a terrible fire in 2019, what famous Paris cathedral was discovered to be the first to use iron reinforcements in its structure?

a) St. Peter's Basilica

b) St. Stephen's Cathedral

c) Funchal Cathedral

d) Notre Dame Cathedral

Answer 30

Paris's 800-year-old cathedral, Notre Dame, tragically caught fire in 2019, but during the rebuilding process, historians discovered that Notre Dame is the first Gothic cathedral to use iron to bind stones together. Historians speculated on how the tall cathedral with thin walls had been able to stand since the twelfth century, and this discovery shed light on the origins of this historic Paris landmark.

Super Fun Facts
For Curious Kids

Question 31

What was once a popular medical diagnosis for women in the Victorian period?

a) Vapors

b) Mumps

c) Swoons

d) Smallpox

David W. Leon
Fun Facts Books

Answer 31

Now completely discredited by the medical community, the term "vapors" was commonly used to refer to a range of symptoms experienced by women, which were believed to be related to vapors seeping out of their wombs. It was believed that women were more susceptible to emotional and nervous disturbances due to their hormonal changes. The vapors were often considered a form of female frailty and were thought to require special care and attention.

Super Fun Facts
For Curious Kids

Question 32

Which of the following animals weren't hunted by people during the Old Stone Age?

a) Mammoths

b) Glyptodons

c) Dinosaurs

d) Megatheriums

Answer 32

Dinosaurs had already disappeared long before humans existed. In the Old Stone Age, people hunted other big animals for food and materials needed to survive. At that time, there were species of animals which are now extinct. They were very big animals called megafauna (mega means big).

Super Fun Facts
For Curious Kids

Question 33

Phrases like, "Arrr, ye scallywags," are uttered during what informal, unofficial holiday in the United States?

a) Bastille Day

b) Three Kings Day

c) Burn's Day

d) Talk Like a Pirate Day

David W. Leon
Fun Facts Books

Answer 33

A favorite holiday for internet users, "Talk Like a Pirate Day" is celebrated on September 19th each year. The first "Talk Like a Pirate Day" was celebrated in 1995, but it didn't gain popularity until humorist Dave Barry wrote about it in 2002.

Super Fun Facts
For Curious Kids

Question 34

Casa Herradura has been producing its famous tequila for over 180 years in which Mexican town?

a) Mexico City

b) Jalisco

c) Puebla

d) Puerto Vallarta

Answer 34

Tourists and tequila lovers can travel to the city of Jalisco, Mexico, and see the family's famous vodka production. Casa Herradura was originally called Hacienda San José del Refugio when it was a high-walled compound where many persecuted Catholics hid from the authorities. Now the site's tequila production is recognized as one of the best in the world.

Super Fun Facts
For Curious Kids

Question 35

While there are many types of vegetarians, what are the strictest vegetarians called?

a) Pescatarian

b) Flexitarian

c) Vegan

d) Ovo-Vegetarian

Answer 35

Of all vegetarians, vegans follow the strictest plant-based only diet, excluding all animal products from their diet, including meat, poultry, fish, eggs, dairy, and honey. They avoid using or wearing animal-derived products. The most common type of vegetarians is lacto-ovo vegetarians who avoid meat, poultry, and fish but include dairy products (lacto) and eggs (ovo) in their diet. Flexitarians primarily follow a vegetarian diet but occasionally consume meat or fish.

Super Fun Facts
For Curious Kids

Question 36

The Industrial Revolution brought hundreds of inventions that changed people's lives forever. Which of the following was invented before the Industrial Revolution?

a) Dynamite

b) Trains

c) Electricity

d) Gunpowder

David W. Leon
Fun Facts Books

Answer 36

In the 15th century, gunpowder was invented. It is thought to have been created by the Chinese, although it is likely that gunpowder wasn't intended for firearms. Instead, they used it to illuminate the night sky by creating fireworks.

Super Fun Facts
For Curious Kids

Question 37

What public holiday is celebrated immediately after Christmas in Great Britain, Australia, New Zealand, Canada, and other Commonwealth countries?

a) Armenian Christmas

b) St. Lucia's Day

c) Boxing Day

d) Day of Candles

David W. Leon
Fun Facts Books

Answer 37

Celebrated on December 26th, Boxing Day was originally a day for the service class to give and receive gifts after wealthy households finished celebrating Christmas. Servants and tradespeople would be given small gifts or time off, and charity donations were encouraged on this day. Modern Boxing Day in the British commonwealth is more like Black Friday in the United States because it is the day that shops offer huge sales.

Super Fun Facts
For Curious Kids

Question 38

Mardi Gras is celebrated before the start of which religious occurrence in New Orleans?

a) Lent

b) Christmas

c) Thanksgiving

d) Easter

David W. Leon
Fun Facts Books

Answer 38

Although Mardi Gras has evolved into a week-long festival in New Orleans, the term "Mardi Gras" really refers to "Fat Tuesday," the Tuesday before the beginning of Lent. While New Orleans has America's most famous Mardi Gras celebration, it is also celebrated in Spain, France, Germany, and England.

Super Fun Facts
For Curious Kids

Question 39

What country launched the first spacecraft into space?

a) The United States

b) China

c) Great Britain

d) The Soviet Union

David W. Leon
Fun Facts Books

Answer 39

On April 12, 1961, the Soviet Union (now Russia) launched Vostok I into space. For 108 minutes, cosmonaut Yuri Gagarin orbited the Earth in the first manned space flight.

Super Fun Facts
For Curious Kids

Question 40

Where did the Iroquois tribes live before the Europeans' arrival?

a) In Canada and the US

b) In Mexico and Honduras

c) In Brazil and Paraguay

d) In India and parts of China

Answer 40

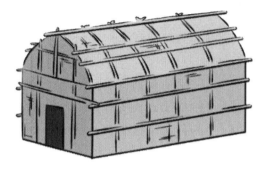

The Iroquois tribes lived in the northeastern region of North America. Today, those territories belong to Canada and the United States. It was the French who named them "Iroquois," but the native people called themselves Haudenosaunee. It means "people of the Longhouse".

You're almost halfway through!

If you've made it this far, I assume you are a true smartie who is willing to learn new things.

Remember, it is totally fine to not get every question right. This game is designed to stretch your mind and teach you new facts from around the world and throughout time!

If you have 2 minutes before the next level, providing feedback will greatly help me for writing future books and will also help other readers when looking at this book.

What do you think of the book so far?

Open the camera app on your phone
Hold phone so the QR Code appears in view
Tap the pop-up link for the QR Code

Level 3

Seize The Day
Like It's The Last Slice Of Pizza

Questions 41-60

Even Things That Seem So Small Can Make
Such Big Changes To The World!

Super Fun Facts
For Curious Kids

Question 41

What holiday was initially created by President Woodrow Wilson in 1918?

a) Labor Day

b) Veteran's Day

c) Memorial Day

d) Pioneer Day

Answer 41

World War I, often called "The War to End All Wars," ended on the eleventh hour of the eleventh day of the eleventh month in 1919. To remember the end of the war, President Wilson declared November 11th a holiday to remember those who died in service of the United States. In 1975, President Gerald Ford made Veteran's Day a national holiday.

Super Fun Facts
For Curious Kids

Question 42

What famous Chinese landmark was built in 1406 as a home for the Imperial family?

a) The Summer Palace

b) The Forbidden City

c) Potala Palace

d) Drepung Monastery

Answer 42

Built in 1406 during the Ming Dynasty, the Forbidden City sits in what is now Shanghai. The palace was off-limits to everyone except the Imperial family for over 500 years. In 1925, it opened its doors to the public as a museum and is a UNESCO World Heritage site because it has the largest collection of preserved wooden buildings.

Super Fun Facts
For Curious Kids

Question 43

Which part of the human body gets replaced every month?

a) Toenails

b) Skin

c) Liver

d) Hair

Answer 43

On average, it takes about 28 to 30 days for the skin to complete a full cycle of cell turnover. It's important to note that the rate of skin cell turnover can vary in different parts of the body. For example, the skin on the face and hands tends to have a faster turnover rate compared to areas like the arms or legs.

Super Fun Facts
For Curious Kids

Question 44

The first colony settled in Canada by Europeans was the current city of Québec. Where were these settlers from?

a) England

b) Spain

c) Holland

d) France

Answer 44

John Cabot, an Italian navigator who worked for the English king, was the first to arrive in Canadian lands in the 1400s. However, the first colonies were established many years later by the French in 1604. The name came from the Iroquoian word Kanata, which means "village".

Super Fun Facts
For Curious Kids

Question 45

What do Christians in Spain and Latin America call the Twelfth Day of Christmas?

a) Julenisse

b) Bom Natal

c) Epiphany Day

d) Babbo Natale

Answer 45

January 6th, commonly known as the twelfth day of Christmas, is called both "Three Kings Day" and "Epiphany Day." Inspired by the Three Wisemen in the Nativity story, children leave their shoes out for the three wisemen to fill with presents.

Super Fun Facts
For Curious Kids

Question 46

Which Peruvian trail reaches 13,828 feet high and must be hiked with a local guide?

a) The Incan Trail

b) Fitz Roy Trek

c) Bay of Fires

d) Lost City Trek

Answer 46

While historians aren't sure why the Incas abandoned the site of Machu Picchu, the Inca Trail is a moderate hike to the legendary ruins. It typically takes four days for hikers to navigate the Inca Trail, reaching its highest peak, known as Dead Woman's Pass, at 13,828 feet (4,215 meters).

Super Fun Facts
For Curious Kids

Question 47

What is the name of the world's hottest pepper?

a) Carolina Reaper

b) Ghost Pepper

c) Banana Pepper

d) Naga Viper

Answer 47

On the Scoville scale, which measures the heat of peppers, the Carolina Reaper averages around 1.5 million Scoville Heat Units (SHU), with some individual peppers reaching over 2 million SHU. It is an extremely spicy pepper and should be handled with caution.

Super Fun Facts
For Curious Kids

Question 48

Which North American native nation lived in the region between the Rocky Mountains and the Mississippi River, the Great Lakes, and the Gulf of Mexico?

a) The Nahuálts

b) The Sioux

c) The Inuits

d) The Selk'nam

Answer 48

The Sioux lived in the Great Plains. Many of them were nomadic tribes who moved to follow the buffalo herds but also established trading relationships with other tribes. Others were semisedentary and lived near the woods, fishing, gathering, and cultivating corn.

Super Fun Facts
For Curious Kids

Question 49

What holiday is celebrated in France on July 14th?

a) Bastille Day

b) Assumption Day

c) Labor Day

d) Armistice Day

Answer 49

Commemorating the day that French peasants stormed the Bastille prison and brought down France's Old Republic, Bastille Day is now a national holiday in France. Dancing and fireworks are a popular way to celebrate while Paris celebrates with a military parade on the Champs-Elysées.

Super Fun Facts
For Curious Kids

Question 50

What Memphis home has half a million visitors each year, making it one of the most-visited homes in the United States?

a) Monticello

b) Falling Water

c) Graceland

d) Longwood Mansion

Answer 50

Now a national landmark, 22-year-old Elvis Presley bought Graceland in 1957. Both Elvis and his mother are buried in Graceland's Meditation Garden.

Super Fun Facts
For Curious Kids

Question 51

What is the name of the virtual assistant developed by Apple?

a) Lulu

b) Ashley

c) Leslie

d) Siri

Answer 51

One of the first widely used-AI models, Siri is an AI-powered voice assistant that is integrated into Apple devices. Users can interact with Siri using voice commands to perform various tasks, including setting reminders, sending messages, making calls, searching the web, and controlling smart home devices.

Super Fun Facts
For Curious Kids

Question 52

The Olympic Games originated in ancient Greece. Athletes from different polis—ancient cities—went to Olympia to compete in several sports. Which of the following wasn't one of them?

a) Wrestling

b) Running

c) Swimming

d) Jumping

Answer 52

Although modern athletes compete in 40 different sports, ancient games had many fewer events. Ancient Olympic games only allowed men to compete and the disciplines "included running, long jump, shot put, javelin, boxing, pankration, and equestrian events". This means that there weren't any swimming competitions.

Super Fun Facts
For Curious Kids

Question 53

What is Thanksgiving called in South Korea?

a) Chuseok

b) Seollal

c) Eorininal

d) Hangeulnal

Answer 53

Typically a three-day holiday, Chuseok is celebrated with foods made especially for the day, including songpyeon, a food made of rice dough that is kneaded into round shapes and filled with sesame seeds, chestnuts, and red beans. Another popular Chuseok food is "SPAM," an American food made of salty, processed pork.

Super Fun Facts
For Curious Kids

Question 54

Which German museum celebrates the automobile built by Carl Benz in 1886?

a) Mercedes-Benz Museum

b) BMW Welt and Museum

c) Porsche Museum

d) Audi Museum

Answer 54

With nine levels and 1500 exhibits, the Mercedes-Benz Museum in Stuttgart, Germany, celebrates one of the first cars ever built. Approximately 150 vehicles are on display, from the first versions of the Mercedes-Benz to racing cars.

Super Fun Facts
For Curious Kids

Question 55

What is the formula for water?

a) H_2O

b) HCI

c) NH_3

d) HNO_3

Answer 55

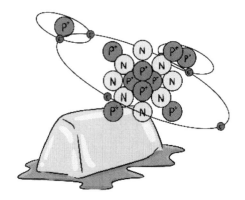

One of the most plentiful and essential chemical compounds, water is made of two hydrogen atoms, each linked by a single chemical bond to an oxygen atom (H_2O). Despite its simple structure, water is a highly adaptable compound that melts at 100° Celsius and freezes at 0° Celsius.

Super Fun Facts
For Curious Kids

Question 56

Ancient civilizations learned to manipulate several metals. Native American people also used another type of material obtained from trees. What was it?

a) Papyrus

b) Oil

c) Plastic

d) Rubber

Answer 56

Native Americans did learn to manipulate metals, but they also knew rubber. This material is drawn from a type of tree that grows in some areas of the continent. The Olmecs in Mexico and the tribes in the Amazon made balls with rubber and used them to play a sport very similar to modern soccer.

Super Fun Facts
For Curious Kids

Question 57

What does the Japanese holiday "Kodomo No Hi" celebrate?

a) Dogs

b) Trees

c) Mothers

d) Children

Answer 57

On March 3, 1948, Japan established Kodomo No Hi as a holiday to celebrate children. While it has been celebrated in Japan since 600 A.D, the modern version is meant to celebrate each child's individuality and their happiness.

Super Fun Facts
For Curious Kids

Question 58

Which French museum is devoted to visual art produced in the 20th and 21st centuries?

a) Je de Paume

b) Pompidou Centre

c) The National Gallery

d) The Louvre

Answer 58

Founded by composer Pierre Boulez and featuring a center for industrial design, a film museum, and the Centre for Musical and Acoustical Research, the Pompidou Centre in Paris is named after French president Georges Pompidou. Opened in 1977, the museum features an unusual industrial design of brightly colored exterior pipes and exposed services.

Super Fun Facts
For Curious Kids

Question 59

What answer is NOT a reason we have eyebrows?

a) Communication

b) Protection

c) Identification

d) Vision Enhancement

Answer 59

One of the primary functions of eyebrows is to protect our eyes from sweat, rain, and debris. Eyebrows also play a crucial role in non-verbal communication and facial expression and contribute to conveying emotions, such as surprise, anger, or happiness. While distinctive eyebrows may help us identify someone, they don't pay any role in enhancing our vision.

Super Fun Facts
For Curious Kids

Question 60

Which of the following inventions was created long before the Industrial Revolution?

a) Matches

b) The pencil

c) The bicycle

d) Vaccines

Answer 60

Modern pencils were invented in 1564, two centuries before the Industrial Revolution. They had a wooden case with a bar of graphite inside, which left lines on the paper. The invention came after people discovered a big graphite deposit in England and realized the material left a dark mark.

Level 4
Who Is The Einstein In Your Family?

Questions 61-80

Have You Tried Testing Your Family Members With This Game?

See Who Can Get The Most Questions Right In This Next Level!

Super Fun Facts
For Curious Kids

Question 61

For how many nights is the Christmas holiday of Las Posadas celebrated?

a) Two

b) Five

c) Seven

d) Nine

Answer 61

A Christmas festival celebrated by Latino communities in the United States, Las Posadas is celebrated for nine nights to commemorate the journey Mary and Joseph made while looking for shelter. The nine nights are meant to symbolize the nine months that Mary was pregnant. During the nine nights of festivities, participants celebrate with food and the breaking of piñata, a papier-mâché container usually holding candies or treats.

Super Fun Facts
For Curious Kids

Question 62

What Missouri monument was designed to commemorate the westward expansion of the United States?

a) Liberty Memorial

b) Gateway Arch

c) Shelley House

d) White Haven

Answer 62

Recognized as a national landmark, the Gateway Arch in St. Louis, Missouri, has a tram ride to the top of the arch for a spectacular view of the city. The building of the Gateway Arch cost thirteen million dollars. It is 630 feet (192 meters) tall and is often referred to as the "Gateway to the West".

Super Fun Facts
For Curious Kids

Question 63

What bird can turn its head 270 degrees?

a) Owl

b) Cardinal

c) Pelican

d) Redbird

Answer 63

Owls possess amazing neck flexibility that allows them to rotate their heads to a significant extent, although it's a myth that they can rotate their heads 360 degrees. Owls have a significant number of neck vertebrae, flexible neck muscles, and unique blood vessels that prevent blood flow interruption when rotating their heads.

Super Fun Facts
For Curious Kids

Question 64

In which country were all these things invented: paper, fireworks, the compass, and the printing press?

a) England

b) India

c) China

d) Germany

Answer 64

All those things were invented in China long before the rest of the world learned about them. The Chinese invented them between the 2nd and 7th centuries, but Europeans didn't discover them until the 15th century. These inventions brought many changes that led to modernity.

Super Fun Facts
For Curious Kids

Question 65

Which famous poet does Argentina celebrate on November 10th each year?

a) Octavia Paz

b) José Hernández

c) Juan Ruiz

d) Clara Janés

Answer 65

Celebrating poet José Hernández's birthday, Argentina's Day of Tradition (Día de la Tradición) is a holiday that honors the poet's contribution to Argentine culture. While not an official holiday, it is widely celebrated with the main celebration being held in the town of San Antonio de Areco.

Super Fun Facts
For Curious Kids

Question 66

The Cathedral of the Intercession of the Most Holy Theotokos on the Moat in Moscow's Red Square is better known by what name?

a) St. Michael Cathedral

b) Kazan Cathedral

c) Holy Trinity Cathedral

d) St. Basil's Cathedral

Answer 66

Known for its vividly colored domes, St. Basil's Cathedral is one of Russia's most famous landmarks. Czar Ivan the Terrible ordered the construction of the Orthodox Cathedral in 1555, which hosts nine churches in one building. The cathedral's more common name honors Saint Basil the Blessed, a homeless man who was canonized in 1588.

Super Fun Facts
For Curious Kids

Question 67

What is the name for the supercontinent that existed around 300 million years ago?

a) Atlantis

b) Pangea

c) Antarctica

d) Zeelandia

Answer 67

Pangea was a massive landmass that existed around 300 million years ago and encompassed all the continents as they are known today. Over time, Pangea began to break apart, leading to the formation of the continents we see today. This process, known as continental drift, was proposed by Alfred Wegener in the early 20th century and has since been supported by geological evidence.

Super Fun Facts
For Curious Kids

Question 68

Who was the first animal to travel into outer space?

a) Lucy

b) Cindy

c) Laika

d) Anastasia

Answer 68

Laika rode up into space in Sputnik 2. The mission was sent from Moscow, the capital of the Soviet Union, on November 3, 1957. The mission's purpose was to test if living creatures could survive launch and zero gravity.

Super Fun Facts
For Curious Kids

Question 69

What food is considered an essential part of the menu in Scotland on Burns Night?

a) Fish 'n' Chips

b) Cullen Skink

c) Haggis

d) Black Pudding

Answer 69

Scottish people eat haggis on Burns Night to celebrate Robert Burns, the country's national bard. Haggis is a pudding made of the liver, heart, and lungs of a sheep, minced with beef or mutton suet and seasoned with onion, cayenne pepper, and other spices. This pudding is then placed into a sheep's stomach and boiled.

Super Fun Facts
For Curious Kids

Question 70

What is the name of the castle in Romania that is often called "Dracula's Castle?"

a) Corvin Castle

b) Bran Castle

c) Peles Castle

d) Banffy Castle

David W. Leon
Fun Facts Books

Answer 70

While Bram Stoker, the author of Dracula, never visited Bran Castle, his description was based on accounts of Transylvania and illustrations of the castle. Sitting on a high cliff, this castle was a defense line during the 15th century when Romania fought the Ottoman Empire. Now, it is considered one of Romania's most important landmarks and includes a "Dracula's Castle" tour.

Super Fun Facts
For Curious Kids

Question 71

What is the scientific study of the chemical and physical properties of soil called?

a) Geology

b) Pedology

c) Anthropology

d) Botany

Answer 71

Pedology is the scientific study of soils, focusing on their formation, classification, and properties. It examines how soils develop over time through geological and biological processes. Pedology plays a crucial role in understanding soil fertility, land management, and environmental conservation.

Super Fun Facts
For Curious Kids

Question 72

When was the first time that airplanes were used as weapons in a war?

a) Vietnam War

b) American Revolutionary War

c) The Hundred Years' War

d) World War I

Answer 72

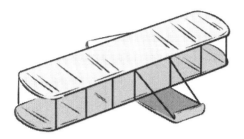

The first airplane was invented in 1896. However, it wasn't until 1903 that the Wright brothers completed the first flight in Kitty Hawk, North Carolina. In 1914, airplanes were employed in World War I for reconnaissance expeditions, and later, in 1915, the machines were equipped for combat.

Super Fun Facts
For Curious Kids

Question 73

What is the name of the Buddha celebrated by Buddhists on Bodhi Day?

a) Siddhartha Gautama

b) Taṇhaṅkara Buddha

c) Sumana Buddha

d) Tissa Buddha

Answer 73

While there are twenty-eight known Buddhas throughout the various sects of Buddhism, Bodhi Day celebrates Siddhartha Gautama (also known as Shakyamuni Buddha). In Japan, Bodhi Day falls on December 7th while China typically celebrates sometime in early January. The word Bodhi translates as "awakened" or "enlightened" in Sanskrit and Pali.

Super Fun Facts
For Curious Kids

Question 74

Which New York City museum hosts both Van Gogh's "Starry Night" and Andy Warhol's famous "Campbell's Soup Cans?"

a) Whitney Museum

b) The Frick Museum

c) Brooklyn Museum

d) Museum of Modern Art History

David W. Leon
Fun Facts Books

Answer 74

Referred to by its acronym "MoMA", the Museum of Modern Art History in Manhattan houses some of the world's most famous pieces of modern art. Over 200,000 paintings, sculptures, drawings, prints, photographs, media and performance artworks, architectural models and drawings, design objects, and films are on display in the MoMa. Film lovers also enjoy the almost two million film stills curated by the museum.

Super Fun Facts
For Curious Kids

Question 75

What is the name of the popular 19th-century pseudoscience that studied the size of bumps on the skull?

a) Ley Lines

b) Feng Shui

c) Phrenology

d) Acupuncture

Answer 75

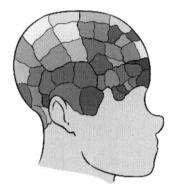

Phrenology was the theory that different mental faculties and personality traits are localized in specific regions of the brain, which can be assessed by examining the shape and size of the skull. Phrenologists believed that by examining the bumps and contours of a skull, they could determine the relative development or size of specific brain regions and predict the person's mental capacities and predispositions.

Super Fun Facts
For Curious Kids

Question 76

Zeus, Poseidon, Hera, and Hercules were gods, goddesses, and other characters of which ancient mythology?

a) Egyptian

b) Greek

c) Roman

d) Mayan

Answer 76

They were all deities of ancient Greek mythology. The Greeks believed in many gods, goddesses, and other mythical creatures such as titans and heroes who lived on Mount Olympus but would come to the Earth and interact with human beings.

Super Fun Facts
For Curious Kids

Question 77

The Muslim holiday of Eid al-Fitr, which is one Islam's major holidays, marks the ending of a month of what activity?

a) Feasting

b) Fasting

c) Sleeping

d) Dancing

Answer 77

The moveable feast of Eid al-Fitr is a three-day celebration that marks the end of fasting during Ramadan. In fact, it is forbidden to fast on Eid al-Fitr, a day when everyone celebrates by eating large meals with family and loved ones.

Super Fun Facts
For Curious Kids

Question 78

What famous waterfall is at the border of Zambia and Zimbabwe?

a) Angel Falls

b) Victoria Falls

c) Gullfoss Falls

d) Sutherland Falls

David W. Leon
Fun Facts Books

Answer 78

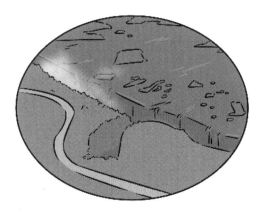

Approximately twice as wide and twice as deep as Niagara Falls, Victoria Falls has a water flow of 33,000 cubic feet (935 cubic meters) per second. The explorer David Livingston was the first European to see the falls and named them after Great Britain's Queen Victoria.

Super Fun Facts
For Curious Kids

Question 79

What is the difference between lakes and ponds?

a) Ponds have rooted plants growing in them

b) Ponds are smaller

c) Ponds are shallow enough for light to hit the bottom

d) All the above

Answer 79

Ponds and lakes are both bodies of water, but they have key differing characteristics, including size, depth, nutrient content, and the presence of aquatic vegetation, so the answer is "all the above." Unlike lakes, ponds are smaller and shallow enough that light hits the bottom. Ponds are more likely to have submerged plant growth, floating plants, and vegetation along the shoreline.

Super Fun Facts
For Curious Kids

Question 80

Ancient Egyptians believed in many gods and goddesses who were embodied as half human and half animal. Who was their most important god or goddess?

a) Cleopatra

b) Horus

c) Ra

d) Jupiter

Answer 80

The highest Egyptian deity was Ra, who symbolized the Sun and was considered the king and father of the creation. Ra had the body of a man and the head of a hawk. He had a golden disk around his head and a cobra, the symbol of power and divinity, surrounding it.

Level 5
Plunge Into The Unknown

Questions 81-100

We've Covered Inventions, Space, Cultural Events, And Traveled The World.

I Hope You Take Your Learnings Further And Investigate More On Your Own!

Super Fun Facts
For Curious Kids

Question 81

What is the name of the sweet treat eaten by people in Tatarstan on the summer holiday of Sabantuy?

a) Kissel

b) Zefir

c) Chak-chak

d) Blini

Answer 81

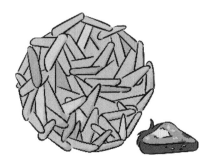

People in the Russian republic of Tatarstan eat Chak-chak, a popular dessert made of fried dough held together with honey. For Sabantuy, large, elaborate dessert displays are created that can be shared communally. Besides sweet treats, Sabantuy is celebrated with music, dancing, and traditional Tartar clothing.

Super Fun Facts
For Curious Kids

Question 82

What group of islands has the largest atoll (a circular group of coral islets) in the world?

a) Bermuda

b) Cuba

c) New Zealand

d) Maldives

David W. Leon
Fun Facts Books

Answer 82

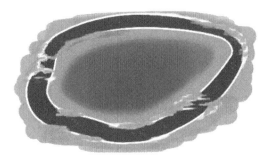

The world's largest atoll is in the Maldives Islands, Gaafu, measures 1034 feet (3152 meters). Famous for its beautiful beaches, The Maldives comprises 1200 individual islands, including some of the smallest in the world.

Super Fun Facts
For Curious Kids

Question 83

Which of the eighty-eight constellations is shaped like a winged horse?

a) Big Dipper

b) Little Dipper

c) Orion

d) Pegasus

Answer 83

Ptolemy, a second-century astronomer, named the Pegasus constellation, which is now officially recognized by the International Astronomical Union (IAU). It is one of the oldest known constellations in the world. In Greek mythology, Pegasus is a white horse that sprang from Medusa when she was being killed by Perseus.

Super Fun Facts
For Curious Kids

Question 84

The Industrial Revolution changed people's lives significantly. What major change helped it to spread?

a) People moved to the cities

b) Most people went to work on farms

c) People moved to America

d) Women could vote

Answer 84

The Industrial Revolution was a process of progressive transformations that changed people's lives on every level. When factories replaced farmland, people had to work there to survive. This compelled them to move from country villages to cities, where factories were located.

Super Fun Facts
For Curious Kids

Question 85

What is the favorite holiday of mathematicians?

a) Pi Day

b) National Puzzle Day

c) National Paper Airplane Day

d) Asteroid Day

Answer 85

Named after the Greek letter "π," Pi Day celebrates the symbol used in math to represent the ratio of the circumference of a circle to its diameter. Why is it celebrated on March 14th? In numbers, Pi averages 3.14. Pi Day is celebrated with pizza (also known as pies), dessert pies, and puns.

Super Fun Facts
For Curious Kids

Question 86

Which forest in England is famous because it features stories about an outlaw named Robin Hood?

a) Redwood Forest

b) Black Forest

c) Sherwood Forest

d) Dancing Forest

Answer 86

Literary lovers are sure to recognize Sherwood Forest as the stomping grounds of the outlaw Robin Hood, who robbed the rich and gave to the poor. Today a visitor would travel to Nottinghamshire and part of Derbyshire to see the pine trees that make up the forest.

Super Fun Facts
For Curious Kids

Question 87

The road system, known as the "Qhapaq Ñan," served primarily as what for the Incan civilization?

a) A route for religious pilgrims

b) An irrigation channel

c) A line of defense against invaders

d) A communication and transportation network

Answer 87

Qhapaq Ñan served as a crucial communication and transportation network, connecting various regions, and facilitating the movement of people, goods, and information. It was a remarkable engineering feat that served as the backbone of the Incan Empire.

Super Fun Facts
For Curious Kids

Question 88

Where did the Industrial Revolution begin?

a) The US

b) England

c) China

d) France

Answer 88

The Industrial Revolution started in England in the 1770s. Manual manufacturing was replaced by mechanized looms and production in factories. The inventions that allowed an increased automation of industrial production were English, including innovative sources of energy like steam produced from coal.

Super Fun Facts
For Curious Kids

Question 89

National Science Fiction Day is celebrated on what author's birthday?

a) Edgar Allan Poe

b) Isaac Asimov

c) George R.R. Martin

d) Ray Bradbury

Answer 89

Celebrated on January 2nd of each year, National Science Fiction Day is Isaac Asimov's birthday. It's also the perfect day to read I, Robot or Foundation, two of his most well-known novels.

Super Fun Facts
For Curious Kids

Question 90

Where in Canada would you travel to see Hopewell's Flowerpot Rocks?

a) Bay of Fundy

b) Hudson Bay

c) Mahone Bay

d) English Bay

Answer 90

Carved from sandstone sea cliffs, the Flowerpot Rocks can be seen in the Bay of Fundy. The Flowerpot Rocks are sea stacks that resemble flowerpots because of how the trees grow out of the sea stacks.

Super Fun Facts
For Curious Kids

Question 91

Where are a grasshopper's ears located?

a) Head

b) Legs

c) Belly

d) Eyes

Answer 91

Rather than being found on their head, a grasshopper's ears are located on their belly. Tucked under their wings is a simple eardrum called the tympanal organ, which allows grasshoppers to hear the songs of other grasshoppers.

Super Fun Facts
For Curious Kids

Question 92

What was the first living being to travel to outer space?

a) A dog

b) A cat

c) A monkey

d) A person

Answer 92

Before trying to send human beings to outer space, the Soviets experimented with dogs, including Laika, in 1957. Unfortunately, none of them could return to Earth. In 1961, the US launched a spaceship with a chimpanzee, Enos, who was able to return to Earth safely.

Super Fun Facts
For Curious Kids

Question 93

What kind of feast do fans of Charles Darwin eat to celebrate Darwin day each year?

a) Moveable

b) Vegan

c) Phylum

d) Religious

Answer 93

To celebrate the author of The Origin of the Species, special dinners called phylum feasts are held by fans of the scientist. A phylum feast is a potluck where all the dishes consist of food not typically found at an ordinary potluck. The goal is to make the feast as biodiverse as possible.

Super Fun Facts
For Curious Kids

Question 94

What is the name of the Icelandic lagoon that appeared in Svartsengi lava field and now features a spa that uses volcanic water to treat medical conditions like psoriasis?

a) Lagos Lagoon

b) Glenrock Lagoon

c) Comino Lagoon

d) Blue Lagoon

David W. Leon
Fun Facts Books

Answer 94

Iceland's Blue Lagoon appeared after a power plant was built on the Reykjanes Peninsula in 1973. In 1981, Icelanders began bathing in the water and touted its healing capabilities. Today, Blue Lagoon Limited has a host of facilities around the lagoon centered on medical research and tourism.

Super Fun Facts
For Curious Kids

Question 95

Both the name of a band and a cycle of sleep, what does "REM" stand for?

a) Removal

b) Rapid Eye Movement

c) Rapid Energy Motion

d) Regular Even Movements

Answer 95

REM (Rapid Eye Movement) sleep is characterized by rapid and random eye movements, increased brain activity, vivid dreaming, and muscle paralysis. REM sleep usually occurs approximately 90 minutes after falling asleep and recurs several times throughout the night, with each REM period becoming longer as the night progresses.

Super Fun Facts
For Curious Kids

Question 96

Who were the Neanderthal people?

a) People who lived in the Netherlands

b) People who populated America

c) People who conquered Egypt

d) People who lived in prehistoric times

Answer 96

The Neanderthal people lived in prehistoric times, about two hundred thousand years ago. Their remains were found in Europe, Africa, and Asia. They used limestone caves as a refuge and made tools and artifacts out of stones, bones, and wood. They created cave paintings.

Super Fun Facts
For Curious Kids

Question 97

What event inspired the creation of World Asteroid Day?

a) The Tunguska Incident

b) Halley's Comet

c) The Dinosaur Extinction

d) Comet Hale-Bopp

Answer 97

On June 30, 1908, an asteroid hit the Tunguska region of Siberia and leveled 2,000 square km (500,000 acres) of forest. It is considered the most destructive asteroid-related disaster in recent history. World Asteroid Day is celebrated every June 30th to educate people about asteroids and how to protect the Earth from devastating strikes like the Tunguska incident.

Super Fun Facts
For Curious Kids

Question 98

What is the name of the New York City building that has a famous spire and art deco design?

a) Chrysler Building

b) Empire State Building

c) Rockefeller Plaza

d) Woolworth Building

Answer 98

Built between 1928 and 1930 and designed by architect William Van Alen, the Chrysler Building was the tallest building in the world until the Empire State Building opened in 1931. The building's design reflects the popularity of art deco and modernism in the 1920s. Since Walter P. Chrysler, head of the Chrysler car company, commissioned it, the building has radiator caps built into the design.

Super Fun Facts
For Curious Kids

Question 99

The center of the universe smells like which of these liquors?

a) Rum

b) Vodka

c) Tequila

d) Gin

Answer 99

Sagittarius B, a gigantic cloud of swirling dust and gas that sits at the center of the Milky Way galaxy, contains ethyl formate, the substance that gives rum its distinctive smell. Spanish scientists discovered there is enough ethyl alcohol to provide everyone on Earth 300,000 pints of beer for a billion years.

Super Fun Facts
For Curious Kids

Question 100

What was the Cold War?

a) A territory dispute about Antarctica

b) Conflict between the US and Soviet Union

c) A war that was fought in the winter

d) A conflict between the US and China

Answer 100

After the end of World War II, the United States and the Soviet Union became the two most powerful nations. Although they never fought against each other, there was a constant threat of a nuclear war. It began in 1946 and ended in 1991 with the Soviet Union's dissolution.

Thank You & Leave A Review

Have you ever tried something scary and new, and it seems the odds are against you? If yes, then you likely know exactly how my wife and I feel right now.

We're taking a leap and trying our hand at writing and sharing our favorite family tradition of trivia night.

Our goal is to create high quality books for everyone to enjoy and hopefully learn a few new things too.

Your feedback will help us to keep writing these books and it would mean a lot to hear from you.

Posting a review is the best and easiest way to support the work of independent authors like us. If you've enjoyed any of our books so far and have 2 minutes to spare, we would be so thankful!

We truly appreciate all your love and support!

Open the camera app on your phone
Hold phone so the QR Code appears in view
Tap the pop-up link for the QR Code

Your Free Gift

Grab your FREE Gifts:

BONUS 1: Our best-selling e-book

BONUS 2: An exclusive, never-before-seen, e-book with an additional 100 interesting and fun facts!

Open the camera app on your phone
Hold phone so the QR Code appears in view
Tap the pop-up link for the QR Code

Check Out The Full Series

Enjoyed the book?
Check out the full series!

Open the camera app on your phone
Hold phone so the QR Code appears in view
Tap the pop-up link for the QR Code

Made in United States
Troutdale, OR
12/12/2024

26353299R20137